HENRY FORD

When Henry Ford was twelve years old, he saw a steam engine. It was very large, cost a lot of money, and did not work very well. Men used it to run some of the machinery on their farms.

Henry decided then and there that one day he would make a better engine — a small one that would replace the horse and move carriages as well as plows.

In this easy to read biography, you will learn about Henry Ford's dream and how he achieved it. You will read about his inventions and the museum he built so that other people could see what he had done.

A SEE AND READ
Beginning to Read Biography

HENRY FORD

by Adrian Paradis

Illustrated by Paul Frame

G. P. PUTNAM'S SONS   NEW YORK

"Dad! Stop the horses! Look what's coming! A steam engine!"

Mr. Ford brought the wagon to a stop.

Henry jumped off the seat and ran ahead. He had seen engines at the railroad station in the city but never before on the road here in Dearborn.

The driver stopped the engine so
that Henry could see it.

"This is used to run machinery on
some of the farms," he said.

Henry asked many questions because he wanted to know all about the engine.

"That's a bright boy you have there," the driver told Mr. Ford. "He should be a good farmer."

Mr. Ford shook his head sadly.
"Henry can fix tools and almost
anything else, but he doesn't like
farm work."

"If we had an engine I would!"
Henry said. He was taller than many
twelve-year-old boys and had a
quick smile.

Then and there Henry had a
dream but he did not tell his father.
He would make a smaller engine so
farmers could use it in place of
horses.

His engine would pull wagons and
make farm work easier. And best of
all, it would move a carriage faster
than any horse could.

A few days later Mr. Ford gave
Henry a watch. That night the boy
took out the parts to see what made
the watch run. Before he went to
bed he had put them back and had
the watch working.

The next day after school he called
on some of the neighbors.

"Any watches or clocks that need
fixing?" he asked.

Many people showed him their broken clocks, which he fixed in no time at all.

Whenever he had time Henry liked
to make things with his tools. One
summer he made a toy steam engine.
To do this he used a can, wood, and
other things found around the farm.

When Henry was through with high school, Mr. Ford wanted him to stay on the farm.

"Farm life is not for me," Henry said. "I'm going to the city. I'll work in a machine shop where I can learn more about tools and engines. You can't make engines on a farm."

He had not forgotten his dream of making an engine that would pull a carriage.

The city of Detroit was not far from Dearborn. There Henry found work at a machine shop.

He helped the men and cleaned the machines when they were not running.

The work was fun but he was not earning much money. There was not enough to buy food or pay for his small room.

One night he passed a jewelry
shop. The sign in the window spelled
out the owner's name: James Magill.
A tall man stood by the door.

"Are you Mr. Magill?" Henry
asked.

"Yes, I am," the man said. "What
do you want?"

18

"A job. Do you need someone to help you?"

"Yes, if you can fix watches," Mr. Magill said. "But you look too young."

"I'm not," Henry answered. "Please let me try."

"All right, I'll let you work for me," Mr. Magill said. "You can start right now."

Every day Henry worked hard at the machine shop, learning all he could about engines. At night he hurried from the shop to the store, and worked for Mr. Magill.

One day he read about a new
engine. It burned gasoline and was
not as large as a steam engine.

Henry thought he could make one
too. Maybe it could pull a carriage.
Was this the answer to his dream?

He visited his father in Dearborn
and told him his plans.

"That would be a fine thing for farmers," Mr. Ford said. "Why don't you stay here and build your engine?" Now that Henry was older, Mr. Ford thought, he could help on the farm.

Henry cut wood, milked the cows, and helped his father every day. At night he worked on his engine, making most of the parts himself.

When he was not working, Henry
liked to be with girls like Clara
Bryant. She was pretty and lived on
a nearby farm.

Clara and Henry grew to love each other and at last she became his wife.

But Henry did not want to stay on the farm. He thought that he and Clara would be happier living in the city.

One day he asked Clara, "How would you like to move to Detroit? I'll get a daytime job and work on my engine and carriage at night."

"Anything you want to do is all right with me, Henry," she said, smiling.

27

It was not hard for Henry to get
work in Detroit. They soon found a
small house near the place where
Henry worked.

Behind the house was a little brick
building that would be just right for
a workshop.

Henry was so busy that Clara saw
very little of him. After work he
hurried home, ate his dinner and
went to the shop. It was often late
before he stopped working on his
engine.

Other men were making engines
now, too, but they were too large.
Henry wanted his engine to be small.
A little engine would be cheap to
make and would fit onto a carriage.

"Horses won't always be needed to pull carriages or wagons," he told Clara one day. "If I can make an engine that doesn't cost much, everyone can buy one."

"Then everyone will have a horseless carriage!" Clara said. She

thought Henry was very smart but
some people called him "Crazy
Ford." They said his horseless
carriage would never work.

Sometimes Mrs. Ford would take
their son, Edsel, into the shop. Henry
would play with the child and later
go back to his work. He never gave
up his dream.

At last Henry's engine was ready.
His car was really like an open
carriage with four large wheels. The
gasoline engine that Henry had made
was under the seat.

Now Henry opened the door of the workshop and tried to push the car outside. But it would not go. The door was not wide enough!

He knocked out some of the bricks around the door and soon pulled the car out into the street.

He started the engine, climbed
onto the seat, and off he went. The
car really ran!

"Crazy Ford," he said to himself
and smiled. His horseless carriage
worked and his dream was real!

A few days later the head of the company where Henry worked sent for him.

"Mr. Ford," he said, "I don't like what you are doing. Your car goes too fast to be safe and it may hurt lots of people. If you don't forget that silly car of yours, you must give up your job."

Give up his job? How could Henry
stop working? He had to buy food
for his wife and son. They had to
have a home. But should he give up
making cars? No! There must be cars
for everyone. He was sure that
Clara would not want him to stop.

"I'm sorry," he said, "but I can't
stay. Nothing will keep me from
making cars."

He made more cars in the
workshop and they sold quickly.
Henry raced his cars to earn more
money, but he did not like racing.

Driving a car at high speeds meant
nothing to him. He wanted to make
good cars and keep the prices low.

One day a man sent for Henry.

"I've seen your cars at the races,"
he said. "They're mighty good. Would
you like to start a company of your
own?"

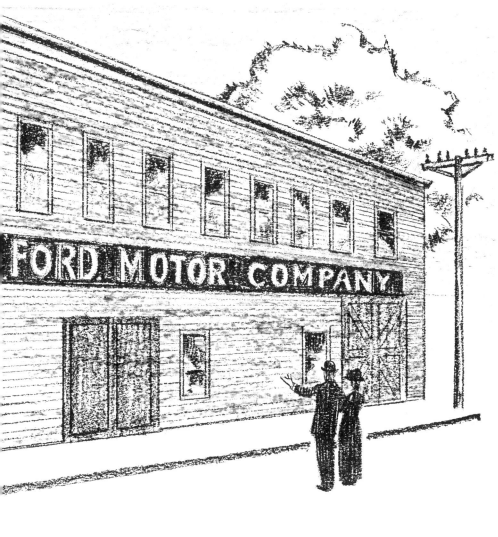

Help at last, a company of his own!
Henry could hardly wait to start.
Others let him have money for his
new company, the Ford Motor
Company.

At first Henry Ford bought his
parts from the Dodge Brothers.
Wagons brought the parts to the
factory and dropped them in piles on
the floor. Three men put the parts
together, moved on to the next pile,
and made another car.

Henry Ford did not like this way of building cars because workers wasted time in walking. Picking up parts from the floor also took too much time. The cars cost so much money that only the rich could buy them. Mr. Ford still hoped to make a car everyone could buy.

"We must turn out cars by the
thousands," Mr. Ford told his men.
"To do this we shall need a big new
factory. I want to make a car a
minute."

The men shook their heads.
"Who can make a car every
minute?" they asked each other.

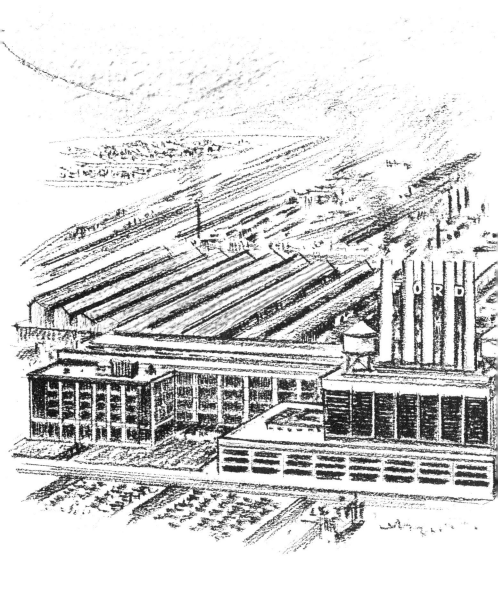

Soon Ford's Highland Park factory opened. It was larger than a small town and there was nothing like it anywhere.

Mr. Ford had made two rules for the factory. First, work was to be brought to each man. And second, no man should have to bend over to do his job.

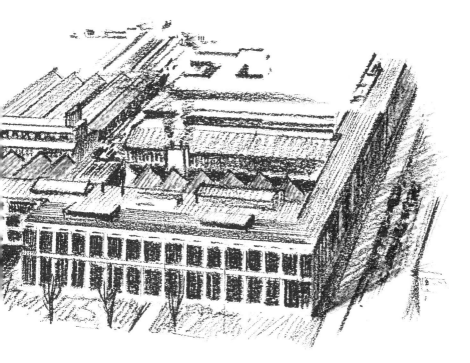

Three men no longer built each car. Now all the men worked on a car as it came to them. No more time was wasted.

A long chain, hung under the roof
of the factory, was moved along by a
machine. Cars were hung from the
chain and brought to the workers
standing underneath or alongside. As

each car came along, some men put
on the wheels. Some put on the
doors and others put in the engine.

When the car was finished, it came
off the chain. Every minute a man
drove a new automobile out of the
factory.

Because it cost less to make cars
this way, Mr. Ford could sell them
for less money. Now many more
Americans could buy the cars, just as
Mr. Ford had hoped.

People liked the cars and many
drivers called them Henry Ford's
"Tin Lizzies." Soon the Ford Motor
Company made so much money that
Mr. Ford became one of the world's
richest men.

Mr. Ford thought about all the money he and the company were making.

"I think we should give more to the workers," he told Edsel one day.

A week later Mr. Ford told his men that he would pay them $5 a day. At that time most men worked for $2.50 a day. Again a few people whispered "Crazy Ford" for paying so much money. But most people thought that this was a fine thing. Now many of Ford's workers could buy cars and other things they wanted.

By this time Detroit had become
the country's automobile city. Many
other large companies had built
factories there too.

As Mr. Ford grew older he went to the factory less and less. Edsel took over the job of running the company.

Mr. Ford had something else to do — to show everyone how people had lived years ago. He wanted to save old American homes, farm tools, books and other things from past days.

First he bought a very old building,
the Wayside Inn, near Boston,
Massachusetts. He had it made to
look just as it did when it was first
built.

Next, Mr. Ford bought land in Dearborn for the job he liked best of all. Not far from his father's old farm, he built the Henry Ford Museum. In this large building he put trains, cars, bicycles, engines, machines, clocks, lamps, and many other things. Here he put his first car and many later cars.

Then Mr. Ford built Greenfield
Village next to the museum. To this
little town he moved many buildings
from all parts of America. Here you

will find the house where Henry
Ford was born. Nearby are the
jewelry store and the small brick
workshop where he made the first
Ford.

You too can visit the Wayside Inn, the Ford Museum, and Greenfield Village. You can also go through the big Ford Motor Company factory near Dearborn.

All this came about because a boy
of twelve saw a steam engine and
had a dream. Because of his dream
America is a better place for each
of us.

Key Words

automobile(s)
carriage
company
engine
drive(r)
factory(ies)

farm(er)
gasoline
machine(ry)
shop
speed(s)
tool(s)

The Author

Adrian A. Paradis considers writing his favorite hobby and indulges in it every morning and evening as he commutes by train to his full-time job with American Airlines. Mr. Paradis and his family live in Yonkers, New York.

The Artist

Paul Frame lives in New York City where he is active in educational work at Friends Seminary. He has illustrated biographies of Robert Frost, Horace Greeley, Lyndon Johnson, and John Fitzgerald Kennedy, as well as *The Boy With One Shoe, Honestly, Katie John!,* and *Casey at Bat.*